TOP 10 MOMENTS IN BASKETBALL

BY NATHAN SOMMER

Minneapolis, Minnesota

Credits

Cover and title page, © Anthony Nesmith/Associated Press and © Mariano Pozo Ruiz/Adobe Stock and © Melinda Nagy/Adobe Stock; 4, © muse studio/Adobe Stock and © Irshaad Majal/Adobe Stock and © Drazen/Adobe Stock and © 103tnn/Adobe Stock and © Gorodenkoff/Adobe Stock and © Monkey Business Images/Adobe Stock and © Brocreative /Adobe Stock and © Lightfield Studios/Adobe Stock and © Benis Arapovic/Adobe Stockand © P.dziurman/Adobe Stock and © Joe/Adobe Stock and © Sergey Ryzhov/Adobe Stock and © alphaspirit/Adobe Stock and © TandemBranding/Adobe Stock and © haizon/Adobe Stock and © Jack Jeffries/Adobe Stock and © Andrey Burmakin/Adobe Stock and © Mariano Pozo Ruiz/Adobe Stock and © Alex/Adobe Stock and © Anna Stakhiv/Adobe Stock and © Holly Birch Photography/Adobe Stock and © BGStock72/Adobe Stock and © WavebreakMediaMicro/Adobe Stock and © Gecko Studio/Adobe Stock and © wavebreak3/Adobe Stock and © Bernard Bodo/Adobe Stock; 5, © Todd Lussier/Getty Images; 6, © Robert Gauthier/Getty Images; 6–7, © Andrew D. Bernstein/Getty Images; 8, © Jesse D. Garrabrant/Getty Images; 8–9, © Scott Cunningham/Getty Images; 10, © John W. McDonough/Getty Images; 10–11, © Kevin C. Cox/Getty Images; 12, © Bill Baptist/Getty Images; 13, © Public Domain/Wikimedia; 14, © Jack Arent/Getty Images; 14–15, © Ron Turenne/Getty Images; 16, © Boston Globe/Getty Images; 16–17, © Manny Millan/Getty Images; 18, © Eric Risberg/Associated Press; 19, © MediaNews Group/Bay Area News/Getty Images; 20, © Nathaniel S. Butler/Getty Images; 20–21, © Scott Cunningham/Getty Images; 22TR, © Bill Kostroun/Associated Press; 22ML, © Lisa Blumenfeld/Getty Images; 22BR, © Noah Graham/Getty Images; 23BR, © Mercury studio/Adobe Stock

Bearport Publishing Company Product Development Team

Publisher: Jen Jenson; Director of Product Development: Spencer Brinker; Editorial Director: Allison Juda; Editor: Cole Nelson; Editor: Tiana Tran; Production Editor: Naomi Reich; Art Director: Kim Jones; Designer: Kayla Eggert; Designer: Steve Scheluchin; Production Specialist: Owen Hamlin

Statement on Usage of Generative Artificial Intelligence

Bearport Publishing remains committed to publishing high-quality nonfiction books. Therefore, we restrict the use of generative AI to ensure accuracy of all text and visual components pertaining to a book's subject. See BearportPublishing.com for details.

Library of Congress Cataloging-in-Publication Data

Names: Sommer, Nathan, author.
Title: Top 10 moments in basketball / by Nathan Sommer.
Other titles: Top ten moments in basketball
Description: Minneapolis, Minnesota : Bearport Publishing Company, 2026. | Series: Top 10 sports extremes | Includes bibliographical references and index. | Audience term: juvenile
Identifiers: LCCN 2025001548 (print) | LCCN 2025001549 (ebook) | ISBN 9798895770627 (library binding) | ISBN 9798895775097 (paperback) | ISBN 9798895771792 (ebook)
Subjects: LCSH: Basketball--United States--History--Juvenile literature. | National Basketball Association--History--Juvenile literature. | Women's National Basketball Association--History--Juvenile literature.
Classification: LCC GV885.1 .S66 2026 (print) | LCC GV885.1 (ebook) | DDC 796.323--dc23/eng/20250220
LC record available at https://lccn.loc.gov/2025001548
LC ebook record available at https://lccn.loc.gov/2025001549

Copyright © 2026 Bearport Publishing Company. All rights reserved. No part of this publication may be reproduced in whole or in part, stored in any retrieval system, or transmitted in any form or by any means, electronic, mechanical, photocopying, recording, or otherwise, without written permission from the publisher. Bearport Publishing is a division of FlutterBee Education Group.

For more information, write to Bearport Publishing, 3500 American Blvd W, Suite 150, Bloomington, MN 55431.

CONTENTS

Taking to the Court...4
#10 Hamby Heave..5
#9 0.4 Seconds..6
#8 The Lynx Dynasty..8
#7 Clutch Three-Pointer...................................10
#6 T-Mac Time...12
#5 The 100-Point Game....................................13
#4 Leonard's Buzzer-Beater...............................14
#3 The Steal...16
#2 The Block...18
#1 Jordan's Last Shot.....................................20

Even More Extreme Basketball Moments...................22
Glossary...23
Index..24
Read More...24
Learn More Online..24
About the Author...24

TAKING TO THE COURT

From neighborhood streets to professional courts, basketball is a favorite pastime of many. The sport has only grown in popularity since the formation of the National Basketball Association (NBA) in 1949 and the Women's National Basketball Association (WNBA) in 1997.

WHAT ARE THE TOP 10 MOMENTS IN BASKETBALL?

Read on to decide for yourself. . . .

#10 HAMBY HEAVE

September 15, 2019 ▪ Thomas & Mack Center ▪ Las Vegas, Nevada

During the 2019 WNBA playoffs, the Las Vegas Aces trailed the Chicago Sky 92–90. With just a few seconds left in the game, Aces player Dearica Hamby **intercepted** a pass. Knowing time was running out, Hamby chucked the ball toward the hoop from about 35 feet (11 m) away . . . and scored! The Aces won 93–92.

There were only seconds left when Hamby took her shot.

Hamby averaged 11 points per game in 2019.

In 2019, Hamby was named the WNBA's **Sixth Woman of the Year**.

5

#9 0.4 SECONDS

May 13, 2004 • SBC Center • San Antonio, Texas

The Los Angeles Lakers and San Antonio Spurs were facing off in a close Game 5 of the 2004 Western Conference semifinals. Spurs player Tim Duncan scored to take the lead with only 0.4 seconds left. That's when the Lakers called a timeout. After the break, Lakers player Derek Fisher scored a **buzzer-beater**! The Lakers won 74–73.

The Lakers went on to win this series in Game 6.

Lakers player Kareem Rush with the trophy after Game 6

The Spurs had trailed for most of this game before the fourth quarter.

Fisher shoots the ball over Spurs player Manu Ginóbili.

Fisher won five NBA championships with the Lakers.

This final play is viewed as one of the greatest in NBA history.

#8 THE LYNX DYNASTY

October 7, 2011 • Philips Arena • Atlanta, Georgia

The Minnesota Lynx had never won a playoff series—until 2011. That year, they won two straight to reach their first WNBA Finals! Then, the Lynx shut down the Atlanta Dream in the second half of Game 3 to win their first championship. The **dynasty** went on to win three more championships in the next six seasons.

Lynx's Seimone Augustus was named MVP of the 2011 Finals.

This was the Lynx's first playoff appearance since 2004.

The 2011 Finals were the first to include teams coached by women.

During all three games against the Dream, the Lynx trailed at halftime.

The Lynx finished the 2011 season 27–7, a best-in-league record.

#7 CLUTCH THREE-POINTER

June 18, 2013 • Kaseya Center • Miami, Florida

The Spurs led the Miami Heat by 3 points in Game 6 of the 2013 NBA Finals. So, fans were worried when the Heat's LeBron James missed a three-pointer. Fortunately, his teammate Chris Bosh caught the **rebound** and passed it to Ray Allen, who hit his own three-point shot to tie the game—with only 5.2 seconds left!

The Heat won this championship in Game 7.

Miama Heat players LeBron James *(left)* and Dwayne Wade *(right)* with trophies

Allen scored again for the team's victory, sinking two free throws with 1.9 seconds left in overtime.

Officials had expected to present the Spurs with the trophy before the Heat's comeback.

Allen shoots the game-tying three-pointer.

Allen scored 2,973 three-pointers during his career!

#6 T-MAC TIME

December 9, 2004 ▪ Toyota Center ▪ Houston, Texas

On December 9, 2004, the Houston Rockets trailed the Spurs 76–68 with 41 seconds left. But instead of giving up, Rockets player Tracy McGrady made history! In just 33 seconds, he sunk 4 baskets that were three-pointers and another game-winning shot. This became one of the most impressive comebacks in NBA history.

McGrady was the NBA **scoring champion** twice in his career.

The Rockets won their final 7 games of the 2004–2005 season to earn a 51–31 record.

McGrady is also famous for scoring 62 points in another game.

#5 THE 100-POINT GAME

March 2, 1962 • Hershey Sports Arena • Hershey, Pennsylvania

On March 2, 1962, Philadelphia Warriors player Wilt Chamberlain broke the record for the most points scored in a single game. He scored 100 points! No player since has come close to breaking Chamberlain's record. It is thought of as one of the greatest accomplishments in sports history.

This game was never on TV.

Chamberlain broke five NBA records during this game.

During the 1961–1962 season, Chamberlain averaged 50.4 points per game.

13

#4 LEONARD'S BUZZER-BEATER

May 12, 2019 ▪ Scotiabank Arena ▪ Toronto, Ontario

The Toronto Raptors and the Philadelphia 76ers were tied in Game 7 of the 2019 Eastern Conference semifinals. With less than a second left, Raptors player Kawhi Leonard shot above 76ers player Joel Embiid's outstretched arms. The ball bounced on the rim four times before falling in. The game ended with a 92–90 Raptors victory!

> The Raptors went on to win their first championship in the 2019 NBA Finals.

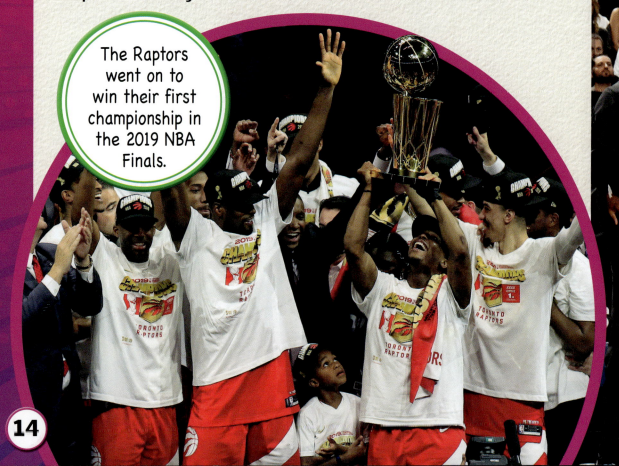

During the game, Leonard scored 41 points, the most of anyone else on his team.

Many consider Leonard to be one of the greatest **two-way players** in basketball history.

Leonard was named the MVP of the 2019 NBA Finals.

#3 THE STEAL

May 26, 1987 ▪ Boston Garden ▪ Boston, Massachusetts

In Game 5 of the 1987 Eastern Conference finals, the Boston Celtics trailed the Detroit Pistons by a single point. Suddenly, Celtics player Larry Bird jumped in front of a pass from Pistons player Isiah Thomas! Bird sent the ball to teammate Dennis Johnson as he was falling out of bounds. Johnson then made the game-winning score with only one second left on the clock.

This is often called one of the greatest defensive plays in NBA history.

The Boston Celtics cheer after Johnson's game-winning basket.

Game 5 ended with a close score of 107–108.

Bird *(left)* playing against Detroit Pistons player Dennis Rodman *(right)*

Bird was a three-time MVP.

The Celtics won this series to advance to their fourth NBA Finals in a row.

#2 THE BLOCK

June 19, 2016 ▪ Oracle Arena ▪ Oakland, California

The Cleveland Cavaliers and Golden State Warriors were tied. With under 2 minutes left in Game 7 of the 2016 Finals, the stakes were high. Then, Warriors player Andre Iguodala caught a defensive rebound and took off down the court. Cavaliers player LeBron James chased him down and blocked Iguodala's **layup** from behind! The Cavaliers won 93–89.

James with the trophy

The win was Cleveland's first NBA championship.

James (#23) blocks the shot.

After James's block, the Warriors did not score again for the rest of the game.

James led the Cavaliers in points, **steals**, and blocks during the 2016 Finals.

During the 2015–2016 regular season, the Warriors lost only nine games.

The Cavaliers became the first team to win the Finals after trailing the series 3–1.

19

#1 JORDAN'S LAST SHOT

June 14, 1998 ▪ Delta Center ▪ Salt Lake City, Utah

In Game 6 of the 1998 NBA Finals, the Chicago Bulls trailed the Utah Jazz by one point. With 20 seconds left, Bulls player Michael Jordan stole the ball from the other team. He used tricky footwork to confuse Jazz defender Bryon Russell. Then, Jordan hit a Finals-winning **jumper** with seconds left!

This victory marked Jordan's sixth time winning the NBA Finals.

This was the most-watched game in NBA history.

The play was Jordan's final shot as a Chicago Bull.

Jordan was named MVP five times.

Jordan (*far right*) shoots the game-winning shot.

EVEN MORE EXTREME BASKETBALL MOMENTS

Many games have been played in the NBA and WNBA. Here are some other exciting top moments in basketball history.

BREAKING THE BACKBOARD
Shaquille O'Neal was known as a powerful scorer for the Orlando Magic. On April 23, 1993, he dunked so hard that the backboard broke!

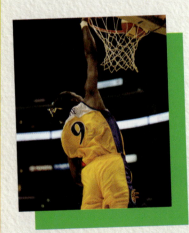

A HISTORIC DUNK
Los Angeles Sparks player Lisa Leslie raced down the court against the Miami Sol on July 30, 2002. She slammed the ball to score the first dunk in WNBA history.

SCORING 81 POINTS
Lakers player Kobe Bryant scored 81 points against the Raptors on January 22, 2006. It is the closest any player has come to breaking Wilt Chamberlain's record.

GLOSSARY

buzzer-beater a score made as the game ends

dynasty a team that remains successful for a long period of time

intercepted caught a pass intended for the other team

jumper a shot where a player jumps in the air as they let go of the ball

layup a score where a player runs, jumps, and uses one hand to bounce the ball off the backboard into the hoop

officials people whose job it is to make sure rules are being followed during games

rebound the catch of the ball after a missed basket

scoring champion the player who scores the most points per game on average during an NBA season

Sixth Woman of the Year an award given each year to the WNBA's best player who is not in their team's starting lineup

steals plays where a defensive player takes the ball away from an offensive player

two-way players basketball players who are skilled at playing both offense and defense

INDEX

defenders 20
halftime 9
history 7, 12–13, 15–16, 21–22
MVP 8, 15, 17, 21
NBA 4, 7, 10, 12–18, 20–22
overtime 11
players 5–7, 10, 12–18, 20, 22
playoffs 5, 8–9
semifinals 6, 14
teammates 10, 16
timeout 6
WNBA 4–5, 8, 22

READ MORE

Morey, Allan. *Swish: The Science Behind Basketball's Most Dynamic Plays (Sports Illustrated Kids: Science Behind the Plays).* North Mankato, MN: Capstone Press, 2025.

Streeter, Anthony. *NBA Finals All-Time Greats (All-Time Greats of Sports Championships).* Mendota Heights, MN: Press Box Books, 2025.

LEARN MORE ONLINE

1. Go to **FactSurfer.com** or scan the QR code below.
2. Enter "**10 Basketball Moments**" into the search box.
3. Click on the cover of this book to see a list of websites.

ABOUT THE AUTHOR

Nathan Sommer graduated from the University of Minnesota with degrees in journalism and political science. He lives in Minneapolis, Minnesota, and enjoys camping, hiking, and writing in his free time.